GRAMMAR FOI

SENTENCE COMBINING

Underpinning Knowledge for Adult
Literacy Practitioners

Maxine Burton

niace
promoting adult learning

© 2012 National Institute of Adult Continuing Education
(England and Wales)
21 De Montfort Street
Leicester LE1 7GE

Company registration no. 2603322
Charity registration no. 1002775

NIACE has a broad remit to promote lifelong learning opportunities for adults. NIACE works to develop increased participation in education and training, particularly for those who do not have easy access because of class, gender, age, race, language and culture, learning difficulties or disabilities, or insufficient financial resources.

For a full catalogue of all NIACE's publications visit
http://shop.niace.org.uk/

Cataloguing in Publication Data

A CIP record for this title is available from the British Library

ISBN 978-1-86201-514-2

Designed and typeset by Book Production Services

Contents

Acknowledgements

My thanks are owed to:

NIACE for their encouragement in writing this book, the second in their series of linguistics guides "Underpinning Knowledge for Adult Literacy Practitioners";

The National Research and Development Centre for Adult Literacy and Numeracy (NRDC) at the Institute of Education, University of London, for funding the research project on which this book draws, and for their subsequent appointment of me as Visiting Research Associate;

Judy Davey, former Research Associate at the University of Sheffield, who led the sentence combining strand of the NRDC research project and read the first draft of the book;

Greg Brooks, Emeritus Professor of Education, University of Sheffield, who brought the potential of sentence combining to my attention in the first place, and was kind enough to cast his expert eye over the first draft of the book.

Introduction

This book arose primarily from the NRDC project I directed at the University of Sheffield, in 2007–08 (Burton *et al.*, 2010). What this research project aimed to do was find out whether various teaching strategies, including sentence combining, might be effective in the adult literacy classroom. A short training course for the teachers to help prepare them to teach this strategy was an essential part of the research. In addition to what we found out in the course of the project, I also bring to this venture decades of experience as an adult literacy teacher, and my long-standing experience of teaching linguistics, including English grammar.

Sentence combining is not a very familiar term in UK literacy teaching, and we will explore what it involves in the first chapter. Its importance lies in the fact that it has been shown to be a more effective way of improving the quality of students' writing than formal grammar teaching. However, this does not mean that teachers can bypass learning formal grammar themselves; indeed grammar provides essential underpinning knowledge for confident and effective classroom practice – and for avoiding some of the pitfalls for the unprepared.

How to use this book

The training sessions I designed for the teachers form the starting point of this book. In these we explored some basic grammatical concepts as well as suggesting ways of delivering sentence combining in the classroom; in turn, the teachers gave me valuable feedback on their experiences of undertaking the training and using the strategy. This venture is also supported by the classroom observations my researchers and I conducted, so that the practice of teaching and learning could directly inform the linguistic underpinning. This is not a grammar textbook per se, although you will be taught all the key terms and concepts you need, and the linguistic information will be carefully related to what is needed in the classroom. In the apparent absence of any other easily available information on using sentence combining with adults, the book will also aim to equip teachers with guidelines for using this strategy in the classroom. It is aimed primarily at adult literacy practitioners, but the basic principles would also apply to other types of English language teaching, including ESOL.

It is probably better to work through the chapters in turn, although they are grouped into sections. The first two provide background: a rationale for sentence combining as a strategy (1); then a brief description of what grammar involves (2). The next two chapters, 3 and 4, examine in detail the aspects of grammar that are particularly relevant for sentence combining. Chapters 5 and 6 describe the strategy in action, with guidelines on using sentence combining, followed by a consideration of how sentence writing can be related to the requirements of the Adult Literacy Core Curriculum. Chapter 7 considers issues of different varieties of English. Each chapter has suggestions for further reading, and several incorporate some 'tasks', with answers, to engage the reader. A full list of references can be found at the end, followed by a glossary of all linguistic and pedagogical terms used.

Chapter 1

Why sentence combining for adults?

The term 'sentence combining' does not seem to be much used in British literacy teaching, but is commonly referred to (in one word as 'sentence-combining') in the USA. By sentence combining, we mean 'techniques of splicing together simple sentences to make compound or complex ones. It can also include sentence-embedding and other techniques for expanding and complicating the structure of sentences' (Andrews *et al.*, 2006, p. 42). In other words, it is a way of making sentences longer, often by means of conjunctions (and we will look in detail later at types of sentences and conjunctions in chapters 3 and 4). It can also be viewed as one way of using a 'writing frame' technique, a point to which we will return in Chapter 6.

Formal prescriptive grammar (modelled on the structure of Latin, a very different type of language from English) was taught from the early years of the twentieth century, and indeed 'parsing' (analysis of sentences) was a compulsory part of English O-level until at least 1960. By 'prescriptive' we mean a concern with 'correct' usage. However a comprehensive review (Harris, 1962) then discredited the notion that the teaching of this sort of formal grammar and associated terminology improved writing (at least for 12- to 14-year-olds) and this led to grammar teaching being abandoned in British schools. Earlier research had already suggested that grammar was too 'difficult' for all but the brightest pupils (Cawley, 1957; Macauley, 1947). Of course, formal grammar is not the only approach to analysing the structures of a language, as we shall see in the next chapter.

However, a misleading assumption had been made at this point that all forms of grammar teaching would be ineffective; more accurately, as yet there is no firm evidence that teaching grammar improves writing, with one important exception – sentence combining.

Research done in the USA in the 1970s and 1980s (Hillocks, 1986; O'Hare, 1973) showed that sentence combining did improve the quality of writing of university students. A recent article reporting on the results of two systematic research reviews showed that, as far as the written English of 5- to 16-year-olds is concerned, teaching sentence combining has 'a more positive effect' on quality and accuracy than formal grammar (Andrews *et al.*, 2006). Why might it be so effective? Perhaps it can be explained in terms of the difference between 'knowledge about' the construction of sentences, and the pedagogy of 'applied knowledge' (Andrews *et al.*, 2006, p. 52). It is also worth noting that Harris in his 1962 study was actually comparing the performance of schoolchildren who were being taught grammar with those who were receiving additional practice in writing. The eminent linguist, Dick Hudson, gives a balanced view of the case for grammar and supports the apparent effectiveness of sentence combining, suggesting that it may be because it involves 'exercises in the production of language, and specifically in the production of written language, so they feed much more directly into the child's growing repertoire of productive skills than exercises in grammatical analysis do' (Hudson, 2001, p. 2).

So far all the research had focused on children's and, to a lesser extent, university students' writing. What about adult literacy learners? When I was setting up the research project, the only piece of research that came to light was an American one from decades ago (Mulder *et al.*, 1978), which gave students of average age 27 with 'less than a high school diploma' (i.e. with less than university entrance qualifications), practice in highly-structured sentence combining exercises. The findings were that writing ability was increased over a relatively short period of time, and it was suggested that sentence combining was particularly suited to adult learners because they already had mastery of the 'underlying cognitive structures' (Mulder *et al.*, 1978, pp. 117–118).

This was the background against which I undertook to find out whether sentence combining might be an effective technique for adult literacy learners in England. At the time of the major NRDC project referred to in the introduction (hereinafter the 'Sentence Combining Project') the strategy was rather an unknown quantity. Earlier NRDC research into writing (Grief *et al.*, 2007) did not report the use of the strategy as such, although it did endorse the use of 'writing frames'. The practitioners who took part in the Sentence Combining Project did, however, claim that they had used versions of the strategy before (although not called as such), at least to some extent, along with other aspects of grammar, such as punctuation and parts of speech. The findings of the Sentence Combining Project were very encouraging:

- The 19 learners (all levels, but mainly Entry level 3 and Level 1) made significant gains in various aspects of their writing, especially sentence structure, punctuation and number of words written.

- This progress was achieved in a very short time (on average only five or six sessions were attended between the two assessments of writing).

- The learners' confidence in a range of language, literacy and learning activities also improved.

- All four teachers expressed enthusiasm for sentence combining and intended to continue using it.

- All the learners said they found the strategy helpful and were keen to continue learning in this way.

We concluded that sentence combining was a strategy that should be taken seriously by the adult literacy profession. This necessitates taking the training of teachers seriously. Even if formal grammar teaching cannot be shown to improve the quality of learners' writing, it does not mean that grammar teaching should be abandoned completely; further research is required to ascertain the value of specific aspects of grammar teaching, but we do know it plays an essential role in the acquisition of other literacy skills, especially for ESOL learners. Indeed grammar is again back in educational favour, particularly with the alleged aim of stemming 'the rising tide of illiteracy in the nation's workplaces' (Cameron, 2007, p. x). Such claims are controversial, but what cannot be disputed is that the meta-language of grammar is part of the essential tool-kit for language teachers, and 'when it is useful and how it can best be used, are matters for teachers' professional judgement. But teachers can only make informed judgements if they have some grammatical knowledge in the first place' (Cameron, 2007, p. x). What this might involve is introduced in the next chapter.

If you want to find out more:

A full account of the methods and findings of the research that included the Sentence Combining Project (pp.11–12, 53–65) is given in Burton, M., Davey, J., Lewis, M., Ritchie, L. and Brooks, G. (2010) *Progress For Adult Literacy Learners.* London: NRDC, which is only available online (free download) at **www.nrdc.org.uk/publications_details.asp?ID=175#**

Cameron, D. (2007) *The Teacher's Guide to Grammar.* Oxford University Press. The Introduction, pp. ix–xi, gives a brief justification for the study of grammar by teachers, and chapter 1 outlines the educational debates on grammar.

Hudson, R. (2001) *Grammar teaching and writing skills: the research evidence.* A useful eight page round-up of research findings. Downloadable from the University College London website – **http://www.phon.ucl.ac.uk/home/dick/writing.htm**

Chapter 2
What is grammar?

Grammar is all about the structures of the words, phrases and sentences of a given language. It can be **prescriptive** (listing rules for correct usage) or **descriptive** (describing language structures without reference to issues of correctness). While linguists favour the latter approach, teachers of English and literacy are more likely to have a vested interest in promoting 'correct' grammar. Have a look at the following extract from the original training materials for the Adult Literacy Core Curriculum.

Task 1

READ THE STATEMENTS BELOW, AND NOTE DOWN YOUR RESPONSES

True or False?   **T | F**

Teaching grammar helps students to read and write English better

Standard English is the correct form of the language

People who speak English as a foreign language know more grammar than native speakers

Local dialects break grammatical rules

Standard English is an accent used, for example, by Radio 3 announcers and the Royal Family

It's wrong to start a sentence with 'and' or 'but' or to end sentences with prepositions

You need good grammar whether you are speaking or writing

The loss of the apostrophe is an example of how the language is declining

Concerns, issues, implications

Reflect on these questions and note down any concerns or issues you feel are important. What is your own attitude towards grammar?

Adapted from: Basic Skills Agency (2001) *An Introduction to The Adult Literacy Core Curriculum. Pre-reading Material*, p. 52.

These statements do seem to reflect a measure of anxiety about grammar; some are contentious, but rather than discussing them in turn, all I will ask you to do at this stage is to note your reactions, and then, once you have worked through this book, revisit this task in preparation for a discussion of issues arising from it, at the end of the final chapter.

There are multiple and sometimes conflicting theories of grammar, which are outside the scope of this book, although if these interest you, there are suggestions for further reading at the end of this chapter. Briefly, traditional rule-driven, formal grammar was being challenged from the mid-twentieth century onwards by other approaches, including 'functional' and 'generative' grammar. Underlying these approaches are: a) a recognition that meaning is central to the structures of language; and b) the fact that all speakers of languages, including children, instinctively 'know grammar' and are able to 'generate' new sentences. As the famous linguist Noam Chomsky put it, a grammar is simply a 'device of some sort for producing the sentences of the language under analysis' (Chomsky, 1957). 'But not everyone who speaks English *knows about* grammar' (Crystal, 2004, p.12). Knowledge *about* grammar involves learning consistent and clear terminology to describe what we know (meta-language). A good starting point is the division traditionally made between *morphology* and *syntax*.

Morphology describes the structure of words, how they can be analysed into their smallest meaningful parts, known as 'morphemes' (e.g. the word 'dogs' can be further divided into two morphemes – 'dog', and 's', the plural marker). **Syntax** deals with the structure of sentences and phrases, with what combinations of words are possible, and how they function in sentences. The focus of this book will be mainly on syntax, as preparation for the strategy of sentence combining, but a brief overview of how the different levels of analysis are organised may be helpful. The hierarchy can be set out in either a top-down (left-hand column) or bottom-up (right-hand column) arrangement, as in Table 1.

Table 1: A traditional five-level hierarchy of grammatical investigation

Sentences which are analysed into:	**Morphemes** which are used to build:
Clauses which are analysed into:	**Words** which are used to build:
Phrases which are analysed into:	**Phrases** which are used to build:
Words which are analysed into:	**Clauses** which are used to build:
Morphemes	**Sentences**

(Adapted from Crystal, 2005, p. 251.)

Some further definitions

The notion of a **word** may seem self-evident, although to linguists it is not. Yes, it is marked by a space before and after in its written form, but not necessarily by an equivalent pause in its spoken version (with scope for humour/misunderstanding, e.g. *I scream for ice cream*). We shall be looking at words again in Chapter 4 when we consider word classes (parts of speech).

A **phrase** is a string of words which form a grammatical unit and which function together in some way and can be replaced or moved as a whole unit. A phrase is built round a 'head word' to which any other words are linked.

A **clause** is a series of connected words which (unlike a phrase) must include a verb. Indeed, as Cameron (2007, p. 90) suggests, all you need to do to find out how many clauses a sentence has is count the verbs. The clause is an essential unit in any consideration of the **sentence**, which forms the focus of the next chapter.

Task 2

Compare the sentence

> Because she was *happy young Maria* started to sing loudly.

with

> Every morning *happy young Maria* started to sing loudly.

Try to explain why the italicised string of words, *happy young Maria*, identical in both, constitutes a grammatical unit or phrase in only one of these sentences. How could this be made clearer?

(Answer at the end of this chapter.)

One final point needs to be kept in mind as we continue our discussion of aspects of grammar – that there is more than one variety of English. 'Educated' English (Standard English) carries more social and academic prestige and is more widely understood than regional and ethnic varieties. The differences between the structures of speech and writing are also significant. Further discussion of these issues, and implications for classroom practice, will be explored later, in Chapter 7. For now, our reference point will be standard written English prose.

If you want to find out more:

There is a useful overview of the issues in Chapter 1 of Cameron, D. (2007) *The Teacher's Guide to Grammar*. Oxford: Oxford University Press. This book is aimed at teachers of children but is nevertheless a helpful addition to the genre.

Crystal, D. (1995, 2003) *Cambridge Encyclopedia of the English Language*. Cambridge University Press. Comprehensive and clear. Chapter 13, *Grammatical Mythology*, is an entertaining account of the study of grammar.

Crystal, D. (2004) *Rediscover Grammar* (3rd edition). Harlow: Pearson Education. The Introduction, pp. 10–35, is helpful. In general, one of the clearest and most accessible short reference books.

Crystal, D. (2005) *How Language Works*. London: Penguin. See Chapters 36–39 for a very clear account of the basics with the 'layperson' in mind.

Graddol, D., Cheshire, J. and Swann, J. (1994) *Describing Language* (2nd edition). Buckingham: Open University Press. Chapter 3 gives a helpful description of traditional grammar, placing it in the context of theoretical grammars.

Answers to tasks

Task 1 will be discussed at the end of Chapter 7.

Task 2

happy young Maria is a phrase, built round the head word *Maria*, in the second sentence. The entire phrase can be replaced by '*Maria*' or '*she*' or moved to the start of the sentence. This is not possible in the first sentence, which contains two clauses: *happy* belongs at the end of the first clause, and *young Maria* opens the second clause, therefore the three words are not all part of the same unit. A phrase can't cross a clause boundary. This would be clarified by inserting a comma after *happy*.

Chapter 3
What is a sentence?

In the study of grammar, the sentence is traditionally the largest grammatical unit of analysis, or building block of language. It consists of one or more clauses.

Task 3

How would you define a sentence? And what do you tell your learners to help them construct a sentence? Note down as many points as you can think of. Discussion follows immediately below.

In purely structural terms, a sentence is a string of words which:

- is complete in that it contains all the elements required by the verb; and

- has internal structure.

At first glance this does not seem very helpful, but we'll unpack these structural elements more fully later. I expect your suggestions also included: begins with a capital letter and ends with a full stop or other major punctuation mark; sounds 'complete' in itself; makes sense, and so on. Invoking these concepts is perfectly sensible, especially in the classroom. However, as teachers, you will be better equipped if you are able to understand various different levels of analysis when defining the sentence.

Sentence constituents

One way of describing the main constituents or structural slots in a sentence is as Subject, Verb and Object (often shortened to S, V and O). Briefly, the subject identifies the theme or topic, and can consist of a noun, pronoun or noun phrase (e.g. *happy young Maria*). The verb can describe actions, sensations or states (not just 'doing words') and can consist of one or more elements, e.g. *see, would have seen* (verb phrase). Of all sentence constituents, the verb is the absolutely essential one. Objects identify who or what has been affected by the action of the verb and consist of noun, pronoun, noun phrase or subordinate clause (see later).

Thus, the sentence *The elderly librarian had given me a huge pile of useful books* can be analysed into the following constituents:

The elderly librarian	had given	me	a huge pile of useful books
S	V	O (indirect)	O (direct)

Note that while some verbs can require two objects (direct and indirect, as with *give* in the example above) others do not require any objects, e.g. *go, fall, wait, happen*. Thus O is not always an essential slot in a sentence.

Another sentence constituent you may come across is what is known as a **complement**. This consists of the word or phrase that follows verbs like *be, become, sound, seem* (e.g. *They are teachers; I'm happy; he seems very angry*) where, instead of describing the effect the verb has (the object), it describes the subject of the sentence, as in the previous examples (a 'subject complement'). Less frequently, the complement can be an object complement, describing the object of a sentence, and usually follows the direct object, e.g. *They elected him prime minister; you made me very tired, I find you extremely rude*. Only a limited set of verbs can take object complements.

Sentence functions

Another way of looking at sentences is in terms of their functions. There are four different sentence types in English, which serve different 'functions' or have different 'meanings'. Compare the different meanings and patterns of:

John baked a cake.
Did John bake a cake?
What did John bake?
What a lovely cake it is!
Bake a cake!

Task 4

What label might you give each of the above sentences? Think about what each means, and try and work out how you know this.

(Answer at the end of this chapter.)

Analysis of sentence functions makes it clear that word order is crucial to well-formed English. *The dog chased the cat* has a very different meaning from *The cat chased the dog*. Other languages such as Latin, Russian or German can distinguish the chaser from the chased using different inflections (word endings or suffixes). Old English was also an inflected language, but modern English depends on word order to a significant extent for its sense. Part of the distinctiveness of the language of poetry relies on the liberties taken with word order.

Finally, we can also analyse sentence types in terms of the clauses they consist of, describing them as **simple, compound** and **complex sentences**.

A **simple sentence** consists of only one clause. It can be as short as *He slept* or even just *Sleep!* or much longer, for example, *The old man slept soundly for many hours in the tiny attic bedroom.*

As we said earlier, it is the number of verbs (or verb phrases) that dictates the number of clauses involved. Furthermore there are no linking words, such as conjunctions, used in any of these sentences – another indication that we are dealing with a simple sentence.

A **compound sentence** consists of two or more clauses, which are linked by a coordinating conjunction such as *and*, *but*, *or*. (Conjunctions will be described in more detail in the next chapter.) Clauses of equal status are linked in a compound sentence, and the conjunction must appear at the start of the second clause. If you remove the conjunction you are left with two well-formed sentences, e.g.

He slept soundly but she stayed awake.
He slept soundly. She stayed awake.

Beware of misleading uses of *and* where it is not functioning as a coordinating conjunction.

Task 5

I'll try and find it.

He went and upset her.

Try re-writing these sentences without *and* in order to clarify their meanings.

(Answer at the end of this chapter.)

In a **Complex sentence** clauses are not of equal status. Here a main clause and one or more subordinate clauses are linked by a subordinating conjunction (e.g. *because*, *when*, *although*, *if*). If you take the conjunction away, part of the meaning may be lost:

> (Although) he slept soundly, he felt tired in the morning.

This example also shows that subordinating conjunctions are more mobile than coordinating conjunctions, as they can appear at the beginning of a sentence, not just in the middle.

It is also possible to write a hybrid sentence, which is both compound and complex, e.g.

> Although he slept soundly and she stayed awake, they both felt tired in the morning and had a row over breakfast.

(which contains a total of four clauses).

Table 2 gives an at-a-glance summary of the different sentence types.

Table 2: The structure of English sentence types

Sentence type	Number of main clauses	Number of subordinate clauses	Examples (main clauses in bold)
Simple	1	none	**He slept soundly.**
Compound	2 or more	none	**He slept soundly** but **she stayed awake.**
Complex	1	1 or more	**He felt tired** although he had slept soundly
Compound-complex	2 or more	1 or more	**He felt tired** although he had slept soundly, but **he got up early anyway.**

19

There are other types of subordination, apart from the type illustrated above, which do not rely on the use of conjunctions; they involve sentence-embedding, and are less central for sentence combining, but may still be useful for writing at more advanced levels. They are described in Deborah Cameron's book (Cameron, 2007, pp. 92–95), and are summarised in Table 3.

Table 3: Other kinds of subordinate clause

Subordinate clause		Examples	Comments
Type	**Characteristics**		
Noun clause	Introduced by *that* (or nothing)	a. I'm glad (that) you asked.	If there's no '*that*' you will be able to add one.
Relative clause	Introduced by a relative pronoun, e.g. *that* (or nothing), *which*, *who*, *whom*, *whose*	b. The cat <u>which stole the fish</u> is very naughty. c. This is the woman <u>my cousin married</u>.	If there's no '*that*' you will be able to add one. Comes after ('postmodifies') the head noun of a noun phrase
Participial clause	Introduced by a present or past participle ending in *-ing, -ed, -en*	d. They stand there, <u>staring</u>. e. They stood around, <u>shocked.</u>	The participle counts as a separate clause because it is a verb form

Task 6

Deconstruction: Look at the five sentences, a–e, under 'examples' in Table 3. Try re-writing each of them as two separate simple sentences; then have a go at combining them again into a different complex or compound sentence.

(Answer at the end of this chapter.)

Relative pronouns introduce relative clauses. The key issue for punctuation is whether the relative clause is **restrictive** or **non-restrictive**. What this means will be explained in the answer to the next task.

Task 7

What is the difference in meaning between these two sentences?

a. The cat which stole the fish is very naughty.

b. The cat, which stole the fish, is very naughty.

(Answer at the end of this chapter.)

If you want to find out more:

Cameron, D. (2007) *The Teacher's Guide to Grammar.* See Chapter 4, 'Sentences' and Chapter 7, 'Clauses'.

Crystal, D. (1995, 2003) *Cambridge Encyclopedia of the English Language.* Cambridge University Press. Sentence functions, pp. 218–219; clause elements and types, pp. 220–221; compound, complex and multiple structures, pp. 226–227.

Crystal, D. (2004) *Rediscover Grammar* pp. 36–65 gives a clearly laid-out account of sentence types and functions, clauses, constituents, etc. See pp. 150–151 for restrictive and non-restrictive relative clauses.

Answers to tasks

Task 4

The sentences function as: 1. statement, 2. Yes/no question, 3. Wh-question, 4. Exclamation, and 5. Command/order. The differences in punctuation are helpful (and in spoken versions would be signalled by differences in intonation). Structurally, the differences in word orders are also significant and help distinguish each function: 1. SVO ('declarative' structure). 2. VSO ('interrogative'). 3. Wh-VS (also 'interrogative'; Note with interrogatives V precedes S, and V can be represented by an auxiliary verb, here *did*). 4. WH-SV ('exclamatory'). 5. VO ('directive' – note lack of S). Also note that these 'rules' can be broken, e.g. *John baked a cake?* where the structure is like a statement (SVO) but the meaning is interrogative.

Task 5

I'll try to find it. (so not a compound sentence)

He upset her. ('went and' adds little to the meaning; possibly a flavour of *He ended up upsetting her.*)

Task 6

a. You asked. I'm glad.
b. The cat is very naughty. It stole the fish.
c. This is the woman. My cousin married her.
d. They stand there. They are staring.
e. They stood around. They were shocked.
Note: These are just some of the possible simple sentences. There are even more possibilities for creating new compound or complex sentences from these pairs so I have not made any suggestions. You will, however, have noticed the changes in meaning that are created in the process, e.g. *Because the cat is very naughty it stole the fish* does not mean quite the same as *The cat is very naughty and stole the fish.*

Task 7

a. contains a 'restrictive clause' and implies that there may be another cat, who didn't steal fish; it identifies the noun as this cat in particular and no commas are needed.

In b., the section between commas could equally as well have been contained within brackets as an aside, as 'extra information' that is less essential to the identity of the noun, the cat. It is thus what is known as a 'non-restrictive clause'.

Chapter 4
What is a conjunction?

We have already referred to conjunctions as 'joining words', the most straightforward way of linking sentences or clauses for sentence combining. In this chapter we will take a closer look at what this concept involves.

You are probably familiar with the term 'conjunction', as being one of the 'parts of speech'. Linguists tend to refer to these as '**word classes**', others being nouns, pronouns, verbs, adjectives, adverbs, prepositions, adverbs. You will probably also be familiar with the way they are traditionally described, e.g. a noun as the 'name of a person, place or thing', a verb as a 'doing word', etc. Again linguists prefer to use a more rigorous system of classification, rather than relying on notional definitions (i.e. defining a word in terms of the 'notions' that are basic to its meaning), which can sometimes be unhelpful or misleading.

Words of the same class will tend to position themselves in a sentence in the same sorts of way, in the same basic slots. Thus any member of the class of nouns can usually be preceded by determiner *the* (unless it's a 'proper' noun). This means that the test of 'substitution' is often used to demonstrate membership of a particular word class, the idea being that you can fill the same position in a sentence with another member of that word class. To illustrate this: in the compound sentence,

He slept soundly **but** she stayed awake.

the conjunction **and** can be substituted for **but** to give:

He slept soundly **and** she stayed awake.

However, in the example we used in the previous chapter, *I'll try and find it*, the fact that this *and* cannot be replaced by another conjunction provides structural 'evidence' that it is not being used here as a conjunction. At the same time we need to be aware that substituting one conjunction for another, although structurally possible, often results in a change of meaning, for example:

Although he had slept soundly, he felt tired.

is rather different from

Because he had slept soundly, he felt tired.

Conjunctions can be divided into two types, as mentioned in the previous chapter: coordinating conjunctions (coordinators) and subordinating conjunctions (subordinators). They are known as a 'closed' word class because they contain a finite number of items: in other words, new words of that class are rarely created. By way of contrast, 'open' classes are 'open' to new items being added. Sometimes the distinction between open and closed classes is described in terms of the contrast between 'content' words (which convey the main meaning) and 'function' words (which express grammatical relationships).

Task 8

Here is a list of word classes (or traditional 'parts of speech'): noun, pronoun, adjective, verb, adverb, preposition, conjunction. Work out which are 'closed' and which are 'open' (depending on whether it is possible to create new members of that class) and divide them into two columns, headed 'closed' and 'open'. With the members of the open word classes, give examples to illustrate new additions to that class. Thinking specifically of conjunctions, what are the implications of membership of a closed class for teaching?

(Answer at the end of this chapter.)

Coordinating conjunctions are used, as we have seen, to link two main clauses (of equal status) in compound sentences; they can also link two words or phrases of equal status, e.g. *my mother .and father* (two nouns), *He is **either** tired **or** lazy* (two adjectives). The main coordinators are: *and*, *but*, *or*, plus pairs, such as: *both ... and*, *either ... or*, *neither ... nor*.

There is a much longer list of subordinating conjunctions (subordinators) expressing a range of meanings. Table 4 is based on Crystal (2004) and gives the meaning of some of the commonest conjunctions.

Table 4: Subordinating conjunctions and their meanings

Meanings	Subordinators	Examples
time	after, as, before, since, till, until, when, while	I arrived while you were out
place	where, wherever	I see where he is
condition	if, unless, in case, supposing	I'll go if you come with me
concession	although, though, if, whereas	I played, though I was hurt
contrast	whereas, while, whilst	I sing, whereas you don't
exception	except (that)	I'd go, except I have no money
reason	because, since, for, as	I can't go because it's expensive
purpose	to	I left early to get the train
result	so	He was tired, so he went to bed
similarity	as, like	Do as I say
comparison	like, as if	It looks like it's going to rain
proportion	the...the	The more I do, the less I like it
preference	sooner than	I'd walk sooner than I'd cycle

Most of the conjunctions in Table 4 are single words but there are several more which consist of phrases ('complex' subordinators), e.g.

as if
as long as
as though
assuming (that)
but that
even if
granted (that)
in case
in order that/to
on condition that
rather than
save that
so (that)
so as to
such that

There are also some subordinators which operate in pairs ('correlative' subordinators), such as:

as ... so
if ... then
scarcely ... when

Task 9

Using the list of meanings in Table 4 as a guide, allocate all the above complex and correlative subordinators to the appropriate meaning categories. (Thinking of examples may help.)

(Answer at the end of this chapter.)

Finally, we will finish this section with a discussion of punctuation, in particular whether a comma is required before a conjunction. Compare, in the examples in Table 4:

I arrived while you were out.

with

I sing, whereas you don't.

and in the case of coordinating conjunctions:

He slept soundly and woke up refreshed.
He slept soundly, but she stayed awake.

In all these cases, the comma is actually optional but tends to be used more often where an element of contrast is involved. The key issue is whether it is needed for clarity, in other words to clarify the boundary between clauses if it is not sufficiently obvious through the use of the conjunction or otherwise. For example, in the sentence

I can sing and dance, and you can only watch.

it can be argued that a comma is needed to distinguish between the first occurrence of *and* (in a list) and the second as a clause divider. For another example, refer back to *happy young Maria* in Chapter 2. Note that it is not the case that a comma necessarily marks a pause in speech.

With subordinate clauses which don't rely on a conjunction as the connective, different rules apply; refer back to restrictive and non-restrictive relative clauses in Chapter 3. (And note that the previous sentence involved a careful use of a restrictive clause!)

If you want to find out more:

Cameron, D. (2007) *The Teacher's Guide to Grammar*, Chapter 2 'Words'.

Crystal, D. (1995) *Cambridge Encyclopedia of the English Language* (1st edition). Word classes and conjunctions, pp. 206–207, 213.

Crystal, D. (2004) *Rediscover Grammar*. For restrictive and non-restrictive clauses, see pp. 150–151; coordination, subordination and conjunctions, pp. 204–213.

Answers to tasks

Don't worry if you found this quite a tricky task – it only goes to show how subtle some of the changes of meanings are when you play around with conjunctions.

Task 9

Meaning	Subordinating conjunction
time	scarcely ... when
condition	as long as, in case, on condition that, if ... then
concession	even if, assuming that, granted that
exception	but that, save that
purpose	in order that/to, so that
result	so as to, such that
comparison	as if, as though
proportion	as ... so
preference	rather than

Note that an infinite number of new words (neologisms) can be generated in open classes, constrained only by conforming to grammatical constraints of word structure (the finite number of prefixes and suffixes) and sentence structure (slots occupied). Email and the internet are fertile sources of new vocabulary. For teaching purposes, in theory all possible conjunctions (as members of a closed word class) can be learnt and, since different endings can't be added, their forms remain consistent. (Similarly, relative pronouns are a finite set with but very few members, see Table 3.)

Task 8

Closed	Open	Examples of new open-class words
preposition	noun	hoodie, quidditch
pronoun	adjective	supercalifragilistic, ginormous
etc. (auxiliary) verb: have, is, did,	verb (main)	is **texting**, has **downloaded**
conjunction	adverb	In theory, any new adjective +ly, e.g. wimpishly

Chapter 5

How does sentence combining work in practice? Some guidelines for the classroom

Because sentence combining does not seem to be documented as a strategy in any teacher training or CPD, it would be helpful at this point to give a few pointers on how it can be incorporated into classroom practice. The following sections are based on the issues that arose in the course of the Sentence Combining Project and are in the form of a series of questions that were raised by the participating teachers.

How do I introduce sentence combining to my learners?

The learners on the project were told that the strategy would help them to write longer and more interesting sentences and so improve their writing. By the end of the project, many learners had also come to regard it as something that went beyond just a sentence-level technique, and increased their vocabulary and general understanding of what they were writing. One teacher said she would also have promoted the confidence-building aspect of the strategy more with her learners; certainly the gains in confidence in writing (and in other literacy activities) were noted by the teachers and confirmed by the learners' own perceptions of their confidence.

It is always good practice to keep your learners informed about what you are doing and why. The extent to which you need to share the technical linguistic terms (or metalinguistic language) with your learners depends on your individual learners and your judgement of them. Certainly, several of our teachers told us that they considered it important to use accurate terminology as a way of empowering their learners to analyse and express thoughts on their own and others' work. As one practitioner told us, 'I always start with the language of it. If you understand the language, you'll understand it.' On the other hand, another teacher welcomed the fact that 'The strategy has released me from being forced to teach all the technical vocabulary. I've found particularly for older learners (over 25) that joining sentences to "make sense" is a much simpler way of teaching grammar.' Similarly, discussion with learners of the way the meaning of sentences can change through the use of different conjunctions is a more meaningful exercise than worksheet exercises on conjunction spotting.

Where do I start?

Since the understanding of what constitutes a sentence is fundamental to the strategy, the obvious place to start is by checking the learners' understanding of the concept. This could be done by directly eliciting the learners' views on sentences – sense, punctuation, length, etc. – discussing these with the class, and writing up the relevant points on a board.

Alternatively, a framework of visual prompts could be supplied, using photographs or PowerPoint. With pictures as stimuli, the learners could be asked to find objects (nouns), and adjectives to describe them, and then, using the nouns and adjectives as a basis, write a simple sentence. One teacher used this framework as a 'starter activity' at the beginning of each lesson to build and develop sentences.

Which learners is it suitable for?

The consensus from the teachers was that all learners from Entry level 2 upwards could be helped by this strategy, with Entry level 3 and Level 1 singled out as deriving most benefit. However, as one teacher claimed, 'Even good Level 2s needed this.' It was found to be harder to involve Entry level 1 learners as much, but there was still scope for oral work on the underlying skills.

Where do I find resources?

The single most popular and useful resource for sentence combining turned out to be the grammar section of the BBC Skillswise website **www.bbc.co.uk/skillswise/words/grammar** which has a series of factsheets, games and quizzes with feedback for the learner. The Talent website **http://talent.ac.uk** also includes resources, although don't try entering 'sentence combining' as your search term as it will yield no results. Many other websites aimed at school-level or ESOL learners offer ideas and possibilities for adaptation. Other well-known worksheets (e.g. abc productions **http://www.skillsforlifenetwork.com/?atk=1287**) can be adapted for use. Another option is to take a piece of text – any prose appropriate for the learner(s) – and 'deconstruct' it. This could involve, for example, identifying conjunctions **and** discussing what they mean, identifying different types of sentences, or even breaking compound and complex sentences into simple sentences.

Another route, popular with advocates of the 'language experience' approach, is through resources created directly by the learners, whereby they generate the sentences to be combined. A word of warning: some guidance or modelling may be needed here, in order to avoid the creation of sentences that are difficult to combine without further adjustments. For instance, an actual example from the project, where learners were given free rein in composing their own simple sentences, was *My name is John. Are we going out for a drink tonight?* (This of course can generate an interesting discussion of why such sentences can't be easily combined.) Having a theme, e.g. using starter picture prompts as described earlier, or writing sentences describing yourself, would help focus the writing; as one teacher found, personal descriptive writing led to some 'creative work' on dating websites!

How might it fit into my teaching plan?

The teachers used sentence combining for different proportions of class time, varying from about 30 minutes to an hour and a half. It proved to be a flexible strategy and could be used as a self-contained element or be fully integrated with other activities. Comments from our teachers included: 'The sentence combining filtered through the whole of the sessions'; 'a very useful framework for teaching other skills – it provided a session structure which could be repeated and built on'; it 'naturally lent itself to extension activities'. Extension activities can, of course, be organised at different levels in order to cater to the differing needs of mixed-ability classes. Sentence combining can also provide a platform for collaborative writing, and one teacher used a paired activity, whereby learner 1 described a drawing to learner 2, who couldn't see it but had to draw the picture according to the 'instructions' from learner 1. After this, sentences could be written describing the two images and comparing the differences.

The next chapter continues the considerations of practical applications for the strategy, with an examination of how sentence combining can fit the requirements of the Adult Literacy Core Curriculum.

If you want to find out more:

For more detail on the learners' and teachers' experience of sentence combining, see pp. 56–61 of the NRDC research report, Burton *et al.* (2010) *Progress for Adult Literacy Learners*
http://www.nrdc.org.uk/publications_details.asp?ID=175#

For ideas for ways of using collaborative writing, see Grief *et al.* (2007) *Collaborative Writing. Effective Teaching and Learning: Development Project Report.* London: NRDC.
http://www.nrdc.org.uk/publications_details.asp?ID=110

A brief discussion of language experience can be found in Burton, M. (2007) *Reading. Developing Adult Teaching and Learning: Practitioner Guides.* Leicester: NIACE.

Chapter 6

Sentence combining and the Adult Literacy Core Curriculum

As mentioned in the introductory pages, the underpinning grammatical knowledge would also be helpful for ESOL teachers. However, the research on which this book is based drew on my experience of training adult literacy teachers and observing adult literacy classroom practice, as well as my extensive previous experience as an adult literacy practitioner. This chapter, therefore, concentrates on the Adult Literacy Core Curriculum and how the strategy can be related to it.

The Core Curriculum does not flag up sentence combining as such (although Entry level 2 does mention that simple sentences can be 'combined'). The strategy is perfectly compatible with teaching the sentence-level skills listed, as we shall see when we examine the relevant elements in more detail.

A recent major guide for practitioners, *Teaching Adult Literacy. Principles and Practice* (Hughes and Schwab, 2010), makes no reference at all to the findings of the NRDC Sentence Combining Project. It does, however, elaborate on the idea of 'writing frames' (p. 225) from the Grief and Chatterton (2007) practitioner guide on writing. Writing frames are also promoted at each level in the Adult Literacy Core Curriculum (see the 'Ideas and suggestions' sections at the end of each page with a link to a pdf) as a 'good way of instilling confidence in a writer … a certain amount of text is provided and the learner completes the gaps with words and phrases s/he chooses'. To what extent can sentence combining be regarded as another type of 'writing frame'? The writing frame guidelines (Grief and Chatterton, 2007, p. 13) mention 'paragraphs' rather than sentences, but do suggest providing 'opening phrases'; 'topics or questions'; 'pictorial prompts'; 'linking phrases or connectives'; and 'suggested vocabulary'. All these would be valid ways of supporting sentence combining.

Entry level 1

Ws/E1.1   *Construct a simple sentence*

Ws/E1.2   *Punctuate a simple sentence with a capital letter and a full stop*

The Glossary to the Curriculum provides definitions of terms, although, under the Entry level for 'sentence', it is misleading to suggest that it usually has 'only one subject'. That would be accurate only as a definition of a simple sentence. Refer back to Chapter 3 for ideas about explaining the concept of a sentence to your learners.

Entry level 2

Ws/E2.1   *Construct simple and compound sentences, using common conjunctions to connect two clauses, e.g. as, and, but*

Strictly speaking, *as* is not one of the coordinating conjunctions (usually regarded as *and, but, or*), and might be better omitted at this stage. The bullet points for this element include:

> *Understand that simple sentences can be combined to make compound sentences by using conjunctions*

which, of course, amounts to what we understand as 'sentence combining'.

Ws/E2.3   *Use punctuation correctly, e.g. capital letters, full stops and question marks*

Here the important point is made:

> *Understand that questions are sentences that have a different word order from straightforward statements*

Although interrogative sentence types can be used for sentence combining, to create compound sentences, note that both sentences will have to have the same structure, i.e. both be questions (e.g. *Are you coming or are you staying at home?*). It may be better in the early stages to stick to statements.

Entry level 3

Ws/E3 .1   *Write in complete sentences*

Here two ways of sentence expansion are highlighted – by 'expanding information around the subject, object, complement and verb', i.e. lengthening a simple sentence; and using 'conjunctions and connectives' to link different parts together. The conjunction 'because' is one of those suggested, and you will recall that this is a subordinating conjunction (for complex sentences), not a coordinating one. In practice, it may not matter too much whether the distinction between compound and complex sentences is carefully maintained, but as teachers you do need to be clear about the difference.

Ws/E3.4   *Use punctuation correctly, e.g. capital letters, full stops, question marks, exclamation marks, commas*

Understand that these are the complete family of sentence boundary markers used in continuous text written in complete sentences

Refer back to sentence types in Chapter 3 for discussion of these different 'boundary markers' and the word order usually associated with them. Exclamation marks can, you will recall, mark two different functions (exclamatory and directive).

Understand when commas are needed in sentences (e.g. to separate items in a list), and that commas should not be used in place of full stops

This last point is very important and is a common stylistic fault known as 'comma splicing', which will be discussed in more detail below under Ws/L1.1.

Level 1

Ws/L1.1   *Write in complete sentences*

Understand that sentences can be joined with a wide range of conjunctions and relative pronouns, and that choosing appropriate connectives enhances meaning

Note not only that 'choosing appropriate connectives' can enhance meaning but that changing the conjunction or other connective can actually change the meaning, either subtly or substantially.

> *Understand that complete sentences should not be strung together with commas to make longer 'sentences' (comma splicing) but should be split into separate sentences or be correctly joined, e.g. by a conjunction*

A comma splice is where two independent clauses are separated by a comma, e.g. *He was very tired, he'd slept badly.* Here the comma could either be replaced by a full stop, to create two simple sentences, or by a conjunction in one longer sentence.

Ws/L1.3   *Punctuate sentences correctly and use punctuation so that meaning is clear*

Clarity of meaning should be the over-riding consideration when deciding what punctuation to use. Over-punctuation can be as much of a distraction as under-punctuation. Omitting all punctuation from a stretch of text and then trying to make sense of it is a good way of demonstrating why and where it is needed.

> *Understand when commas are needed in sentences, to separate parts of some complex sentences or enclose extra information, and that commas should not be used in place of full stops*

Note that commas can also be needed for clarity in compound sentences (refer back to the end of Chapter 4). 'Enclosing extra information' refers to non-restrictive relative clauses (see the end of Chapter 3).

Level 2

Ws/L2.1   *Construct complex sentences*

Understand that complex sentences have more variety of structure than simple and compound sentences and that stops the writing becoming boring

Understand that complex sentences always have more than one part (i.e. clause) and the parts are more closely related to each other than two separate sentences

The same can, of course, be said of compound sentences, not just complex ones.

Understand that simple or compound sentences are preferable for some types of writing, e.g. instructions or directions

Understand that effective writing often uses a mixture of simple, compound and complex sentences

This should be the ultimate aim of the strategy of sentence combining – an awareness of how different sentence structures can be developed, and a feel for the ways they can be used appropriately for different purposes. This is the area of linguistics known as **register**, closely linked or even sometimes used interchangeably with the concept of **genre**. More precisely, register means a socially defined variety of language (e.g. legal, scientific) and genre is the category of literary composition used in the particular context or social situation (e.g. a contract, research report) and we will be looking at this area in the next chapter.

Ws/L2.2/3/4 repeat the requirements to use correct grammar and punctuate correctly as in Ws/L1.

You will see from the Core Curriculum that there is scope for working on sentence combining at all levels, starting with the construction of simple sentences and combining them into compound sentences. As noted earlier, in Chapter 1, the Sentence Combining Project involved learners of all levels, although teachers suggested that those at Entry level 3 and Level 1 would derive most benefit.

In the Core Curriculum, there seems to be some confusion between coordinating and subordinating conjunctions. Remember that coordinators are very restricted in number and can only be used between clauses, i.e. in the middle of a sentence, whereas subordinators can occur at the beginning of a sentence. Compare the following sentences:

> The cat was hungry **and** caught mice.

> The cat caught mice **as** he was hungry.

or

> **As** he was hungry, the cat caught mice.

(But not:

> ***And** caught mice the cat was hungry.)

However, in practice don't get too worried about getting your learners to distinguish between compound and complex, coordinating and subordinating. After all, one of the attractions of the strategy of sentence combining is the fact that you can choose to bypass technical labels for much of the time with your learners.

If you want to find out more:

The Adult Literacy Core Curriculum can be accessed at
http://www.excellencegateway.org.uk/page.aspx?o=sflcurriculum (free,
but requires registration with a password).

Note that the exercises and materials on the *Skillswise* website:
http://www.bbc.co.uk/skillswise/ are fully referenced to the Core
Curriculum.

For useful exercises on comma splicing see:
**www.bristol.ac.uk/arts/exercises/grammar/grammar_tutorial/
page_07.htm**

On genre and register see pp. 220–229 in Hughes, N. and Schwab, I. (eds)
(2010) *Teaching Adult Literacy. Principles and Practice*. NRDC/Open
University Press.

Chapter 7

What about different varieties of English? Issues of dialect and register

We mentioned in Chapter 2 that 'Standard English' (SE) would form the basis for our description of grammar. This is because it is the variety of English that has most prestige, and is most widely understood, not because it is more 'correct' or intrinsically superior. To linguists, SE is just one **dialect** amongst many. The term 'dialect' describes a variety of a language with features of grammar and vocabulary which distinguish it from other varieties of that language, and identify the regional and/or social background of the user. Although dialects often show regional features, this is not the case with SE, which lacks a distinct geographical base. A dialect must be differentiated from an **accent**, which only describes features of pronunciation, although, informally, 'dialect' is sometimes used in a way that includes accent. The SE dialect can be spoken in a variety of different accents, not just in Received Pronunciation (RP), the prestige but, in practice, minority accent. Other (regional or national) dialects of English, however, do tend to be spoken with their related accents.

Distinctive features of dialects can involve different vocabulary (such as *wee bairn* for *little child*, or standard words used with different meanings, e.g. *learn* used in the sense of *teach* (*I'll learn him to behave*). Grammatical features frequently involve differences in negative formation (e.g. *I didn't have no time, He ain't coming*); apparent discrepancies with subject–verb agreement, with such forms as *I seen it, I likes it*; pronoun use *thou, thee* for (singular) *you, us* for *me*, etc. Caribbean dialects have a very distinctive grammatical identity, e.g. lack of auxiliary verbs, as in *They going, How you know?* (Crystal, 2004).

Different dialectal features have implications, of course, for 'correct' sentence construction, but only a few have direct implications for the strategy of sentence combining. Conjunctions are not particularly represented in lists of dialect differences, with the notable exception of *while*, used in Yorkshire dialects in the sense of *until*, e.g. *I'll wait while your taxi comes*. More significantly, relative pronouns, which can open subordinate clauses in complex sentences, can be subject to some variation. Here are the examples given in Hughes and Trudgill (1987, pp. 17–18):

1. That was the man what done it
2. That was the man which done it
3. That was the man as done it
4. That was the man at done it
5. That was the man done it
6. That's the man what his son done it

Task 10

Which, if any, of these forms 1–6 are you familiar with? Which are difficult to understand?
a) Convert them all into Standard English.
b) Give an example of where each linking word used in the examples could feature in Standard English in a complex sentence.

(Answer at the end of this chapter.)

It is important to encourage your learners to write using the most empowering form of literacy, Standard English, whatever their dialects. However it is equally important to be aware that all dialects have 'grammars', in the sense that they all follow 'rules' and they all have contexts in which they are the appropriate dialects to use (e.g. with family and close friends). They are in no way 'substandard' or 'impoverished' forms in a communicative sense. At the same time it is worth thinking about the implications of the lack of exposure to written language that literacy learners have, and how this may reinforce their use of non-standard dialects. Consider what Deborah Cameron says:

> Because literate people treat the written form as their model for all language, the grammar of written English becomes their model for judging grammatical correctness. That, in turn, means treating the standard dialect as the norm, because SE is the only dialect which is used consistently in writing.

(Cameron, 2007, p. 99)

This brings us to a brief discussion of the differences between speech and writing. Even people who normally write in Standard English rarely speak it consistently, even if they imagine they do! Informal spontaneous speech in any dialect can result in repetition, rephrasing, incomplete sentences, etc. Sentences that are uttered are more likely to have straightforward structures, i.e. be simple or compound, using coordinating conjunctions. Complex sentences, using subordination, require a far greater degree of forward planning. This is another argument in favour of starting sentence combining with compound sentences, as these are more likely to reflect familiar speech patterns. It is good practice to involve learners in discussions about dialects and differences between spoken and written language.

Also central to a discussion of different varieties of English is the notion of register, which we mentioned in the previous chapter. Different registers can be distinguished by specialist vocabulary (law, medicine, sport, etc.) and/or differing grammatical constructions, and involve mastery of different genres, e.g.

Newspaper headlines, advertisements, notices, etc. frequently use what can be thought of as incomplete sentences, e.g. *Rioters no better than animals*;

Because you're worth it; *For Sale*, where the 'missing' parts are implied.

Report writing in general, and scientific writing in particular, favour the greater objectivity of passive constructions, e.g. *The classes were held in a wide variety of venues.*

Instructions (recipes, DIY, etc.) use the 'directive' construction – verb followed by object – *Sift flour* **and** *empty into large bowl. Rub in butter* **until** *it resembles fine breadcrumbs.* (Also note the lack of determiners such as *the*.) But you will also note from these baking instructions, in which I have highlighted the connectives, that whereas coordinators such as *and* join clauses of equal status (and therefore involve similar directive construction) subordinate clauses need not.

Constructing sentences and successfully mastering sentence combining will thus also involve an understanding of register and how it affects grammar. Sentences must share features of a similar register in order to be successfully combined.

To finish, and by way of summing up, please now turn back to that very first Task from Chapter 2, based on Core Curriculum training materials. Look again at the notes you made on it. Are your responses to any of the points different now that you have had the opportunity to consider some aspects of grammar in more depth? There are no right or wrong answers but I offer the following by way of commentary on each point:

- The value of grammar teaching is as yet unproven, with the exception of sentence combining. However, awareness of the structures of language and the metalinguistic terms with which to describe them can be a way of empowering learners.

- Standard English should be regarded not so much in terms of its 'correctness' as of its prestige, and the status that can confer. Linguistically, it is just one dialect amongst many.

- All speakers of a language, and of whatever dialect of that language, know (how to use) grammar instinctively (as distinct from knowing 'about' it). Foreign language learners have to pay more overt attention to the learning of grammatical structures in order to master another language.

- Local, i.e. non-standard, dialects have their own grammatical rules, which they follow.

- Standard English is not an accent (pronunciation) but a dialect (grammar and vocabulary). Radio 3 announcers and the Royal Family are not the only people who use the prestige dialect of Standard English, but they are more likely to speak it with the prestige accent, RP.

- Prescriptive grammar is concerned with such issues as correct usage, and attempts to 'freeze' language to stop it changing. All living languages naturally evolve and change. Not only is it becoming increasingly acceptable in SE to start a sentence with 'and' or 'but', or end sentences with prepositions, but email and the internet are accelerating language change.

- There are many differences in grammatical usage between spoken and written language. 'Good' grammar, if it means the grammar of SE, is important in written contexts as this is the dialect most widely accepted for writing. The appropriateness of a dialect used in spoken language, with its associated grammatical rules, will depend on social context or register.

- The 'loss of the apostrophe' is a matter of punctuation conventions and not an example of language 'decline' as such. (More of an issue might actually be the superfluous apostrophe – sometimes known as the 'greengrocer's apostrophe' – *apple's*, etc.)

If you want to find out more:

Burton, M. (2011) *Phonetics for Phonics*. Leicester: NIACE. See Chapter 7 for a brief discussion of issues surrounding different varieties of English and how these can affect learners.

For useful summaries of the main features of different varieties of English, see Hughes, A. and Trudgill, P. (1987) *English Accents and Dialects*. London: Edward Arnold, pp. 13–26; and Cameron, D. (2007) *The Teacher's Guide to Grammar*. Oxford University Press, pp. 107–112.

Crystal, D. (2004) *Rediscover Grammar*, p. 31 outlines some of the distinctive features of Caribbean English.

For differences between speech and writing, see, e.g., Crystal, D. (2004) as above, pp. 20–23; Cameron, D. (2007) as above, pp. 117–120; Crystal, D. (2005) *How Language Works*. London: Penguin, Chapter 23.

Answer to Task 10

All these sentences are intelligible, even if they are forms you do not normally use or hear. The grammatical differences between dialects are really quite superficial – a point that is worth bearing in mind. The hardest one to decode is arguably number 5, simply because 'at' is not a generally recognised connective.

1, 2, 3, 4, 5: That was the man who did it. 6: That's the man whose son did it.

1/6. *I understand* ***what*** *the man did* – 'what' can't refer to the noun immediately preceding it.

2. *That was the dog* ***which*** *did it* – 'which' in SE can't refer to people, only animals and objects.

3. *That was the man,* ***as*** *I told you* – 'as' used as a subordinating conjunction, not a relative pronoun.

4. Note that, in SE, ***at*** cannot be used as a connective, only as a preposition.

5. In SE, omission of the relative pronoun isn't possible here, but can be done in other contexts, e.g. *I can see the man (whom/that) you know.*

49

References

Andrews, R., Torgerson, C., Beverton, S., Freeman, A., Locke, T., Zhu, G., Robinson, A. and Zhu, D. (2006) The effect of grammar teaching on writing development. *British Educational Research Journal*, 32, 1, 39–55.

Basic Skills Agency (2001) *An introduction to The Adult Literacy Core Curriculum. Pre-reading material*. London: Basic Skills Agency.

Burton, M. (2011) *Phonetics for Phonics*. Leicester: NIACE.

Burton, M., Davey, J., Lewis, M. and Ritchie, L. and Brooks, G. (2010) *Progress for Adult Literacy Learners*. London: NRDC. Only available online (free download) at **www.nrdc.org.uk/publications_details.asp?ID=175#** .

Cameron, D. (2007) *The Teacher's Guide to Grammar*. Oxford University Press.

Cawley, F. (1957) The difficulty of English grammar for pupils of secondary school age. MEd thesis, University of Manchester.

Chomsky, N. (1957) *Syntactic Structures*. The Hague: Mouton.

Crystal, D. (1987, 2010) *Cambridge Encyclopedia of Language* (in several editions since 1987) Cambridge: Cambridge University Press.

Crystal, D. (1995, 2003) *Cambridge Encyclopedia of the English Language* (1st and 2nd editions). Cambridge: Cambridge University Press.

Crystal, D. (2004) *Rediscover Grammar* (3rd edition). Harlow: Pearson Education.

Crystal, D. (2005) *How Language Works*. London: Penguin.

Graddol, D., Cheshire, J. and Swann, J. (1994) *Describing Language* (2nd edition). Buckingham: Open University Press.

Grief, S. and Chatterton, J. (2007) *Writing. Developing Adult Teaching and Learning: Practitioner Guides*. Leicester: NIACE.

Grief, S., Meyer, B. and Burgess, A. (2007) *Effective Teaching and Learning: Writing.* London: NRDC. http://www.nrdc.org.uk/publications_details.asp?ID=88 .

Harris, R.J. (1962) An experimental inquiry into the functions and value of formal grammar in the teaching of English, with special reference to the teaching of correct written English to children aged twelve to fourteen. PhD thesis, University of London.

Hillocks, G. (1986) *Research on Written Composition.* Urbana, Illinois: ERIC Clearing House on Reading and Communication Skills.

Hudson, R. (2001) *Grammar Teaching and Writing Skills: The Research Evidence.* Downloadable from the University College London website http://www.phon.ucl.ac.uk/home/dick/writing.htm .

Hughes, A. and Trudgill, P. (1987) *English Accents and Dialects. An Introduction to Social and Regional Varieties of British English* (now into 4th edition). London: Edward Arnold.

Hughes, N. and Schwab, I. (2010) *Teaching Adult Literacy. Principles and Practice.* London: NRDC.

Macauley, W.J. (1947) The difficulty of grammar. *British Journal of Educational Psychology,* 17, 153–162.

Mulder, J.E.M., Braun, C. and Holliday, W.G. (1978) Effects of sentence-combining practice on linguistic maturity level of adult students. *Adult Education Quarterly*, 28, 111–120. Online at http://aeq.sagepub.com/cgi/content/abstract/28/2/111 .

O'Hare, F. (1973) *Sentence-Combining: Improving Student Writing Without Formal Grammar Instruction.* Research Report no 15. Urbana, Illinois: National Council of Teachers of English.

Glossary

Many of these definitions are based on those in the glossaries of David Crystal's two Cambridge encyclopedias (see references). I also refer to glossaries in other publications, including Cameron (2007). Where there is another term in bold within a definition, it can be found with its own entry within this glossary.

accent Features of pronunciation that signal regional or social identity (cf. **dialect**).

auxiliary verb A 'helping' verb that assists the main verb to make various grammatical distinctions, e.g. *is walking, has walked, did he walk?*

clause A series of connected words (a structural unit), which must include a verb. Can be equivalent to a sentence (a **simple sentence**) or can be smaller than a whole sentence (as in a **compound** or **complex sentence**).

closed Describes a **word class** that has a finite number of items and is 'closed' to the addition of new words, e.g. conjunctions. Can also be referred to as **function words**.

collaborative writing Writing done by learners working together in pairs or in small groups.

comma splicing Incorrect use of a comma to join two independent clauses.

complex sentence A sentence with one main clause and one or more subordinate clauses, usually linked by means of **connectives** such as a **subordinating conjunction, relative**

pronoun or *that*.

compound sentence A sentence with two or more main **clauses** which are joined by a connective.

conjunction A word or phrase that joins grammatical units – words, clauses or sentences; can be **coordinating** or **subordinating**. Sometimes known as a **connective** although strictly speaking a conjunction is only one type of connective.

connective A word or phrase that links grammatical units – includes **conjunctions**.

content word A word that has an independent 'dictionary' meaning (cf. **function word**).

coordinating conjunction (coordinator) Links clauses of equal status (e.g. *and, but, or*).

descriptive grammar Account of a language's structure which aims to describe objectively how the language is used in practice (cf. **prescriptive grammar**).

dialect A language variety in which use of grammar and vocabulary identifies the regional or social background of the user (cf. **accent**).

function word A word whose main role is to express a grammatical relationship, rather than an independent meaning (cf. **content word**).

functional grammar Approach that considers how the structures of a language are used to express given meanings.

generative grammar Set of formal rules to generate the infinite set of sentences possible in a language (associated with the influential American linguist, Noam Chomsky).

genre An identifiable category of written composition, characterized often by distinctive language and conventions, e.g. report, novel.

head word The main word in a phrase; the word a phrase is built round.

inflection Change in a word to indicate a grammatical distinction, such as tense or number. In English, often a suffix, e.g *walking*, *girl's*. (These two words can be described as 'inflected'.)

language experience An approach to teaching and learning which involves helping the learners transcribe their own writing.

meta-language A language used for talking about language. 'Metalinguistic' is the adjective to describe such a language.

morpheme The smallest unit of grammar, i.e. the smallest meaningful part of a **word**, not capable of being divided further.

morphology The branch of grammar which analyses the internal structure of words and how they can be analysed into **morphemes** (cf. **syntax**).

non-restrictive relative clause Provides optional information which does not affect the identity of the noun it describes (cf. **restrictive relative clause**).

notional Defines a grammatical unit in terms of its meaning rather than its form.

open Describes a **word class** which is 'open' to the addition of new members, e.g. noun (cf. **closed**).

part of speech Another term for **word class**.

participle Verb form, ending in *-ing, -ed or -en.* Can be used with **auxiliary verbs**.

phrase A string of words which form a grammatical unit; smaller than a clause and need not contain a verb.

prescriptive grammar Account of a language's structure that aims to define 'correct' usage (cf. **descriptive grammar**).

register Socially defined variety of language, often distinguished by specialist vocabulary.

relative clause A type of subordinate (not 'main') clause, introduced by a **relative pronoun.**

relative pronoun A pronoun that introduces a **relative clause**; refers back to ('relates' to) the noun it follows, e.g. I see the man *who* lost his umbrella (*who lost his umbrella* is the relative clause, referring back to *the man*).

restrictive relative clause Identifies what the noun is referring to, 'restricts' its meaning, and is contained within commas (cf. **non-restrictive relative clause**).

RP (Received Pronunciation) Regionally neutral prestige **accent** of British English, sometimes known as 'BBC English'; usually associated with the **dialect** known as **Standard English (SE).**

sentence Grammatical unit consisting of one or more clauses. Has internal structure and is complete in itself. In writing is conventionally enclosed between a capital letter and a full stop.

sentence combining (or **sentence-combining**) Technique for expanding sentence structure by creating **compound** and **complex** sentences from **simple** sentences.

simple sentence A sentence that consists of only one clause; has only one verb.

Standard English (SE) The 'educated' dialect of British English, geographically neutral, used in formal writing.

subordinating conjunction (subordinator) Opens a subordinate clause (e.g. *because, if, although*).

syntax The branch of grammar which analyses sentence structure and word order (cf. **morphology**).

word The smallest unit of grammar that can stand alone as an utterance; consists of one or more **morphemes** and in written language is separated by spaces.

word class Set of words defined by grammatical characteristics, i.e. members of the same class share the same features, e.g. nouns can be preceded by *'the'* and take suffix –s to indicate plural. Word classes can be **open** or **closed**. Also known as **parts of speech** and defined in **notional** terms.

writing frame A way of supporting or 'scaffolding' learners' writing by supplying structured prompts, e.g. opening phrases, pictorial prompts, connectives, etc.